The Bru
Brunel and Other Things

by

Ken Andrews

BIAS *histories* No 5

BIAS *walks* No 1

"The Brunel Walk"

Brunel and Other Things

Published by

Bristol Industrial Archaeological Society

2013

ISBN 978-1-908905-04-8

The information in this BIAS *histories* is correct as of December 2012. Neither the Bristol Industrial Archaeological Society nor the author can accept liability for any claims from readers and others following this guided walk.

The Brunel Walk :

Brunel and Other Things

A Linear Walk of about 3 miles. The Walk may be taken in two parts: Temple Meads to SS Great Britain and SS Great Britain to Cumberland Basin.

The Walk begins in Temple Gate at the bottom of the Station incline. Walk up the incline, passing the former offices of the Bristol Exeter Railway.

Bristol and Exeter Office Building

At the top of the incline is the 1870s Digby Wyatt Terminus.

Digby Wyatt 1870s terminus

Enter the station through the left hand small doorway and turn left, following the Ferry and Temple Quay signs leading into the car park. This was formerly Brunel's 1841 Great Western train station with its mock hammer beam roof construction.

Brunel's Train Station

Exit the car park following the Ferry and Temple Quay signs, along Isambard Walk to the Square. Walk diagonally across the Square.

Walk across the Square to Temple Back East

Then go down Temple Back East until you reach the statue of Brunel, passing Rivergate on your left. The bronze sculpture of Brunel by John Doubleday was originally erected looking towards the waterway on the City Centre in 1982. At the same time a counterpart was erected at Paddington Station. It was moved to its current position by Brunel's solicitors, Osborne Clark, in 2006, which was the bi-centenary of his birth.

I K Brunel

Retrace your steps and walk along Rivergate, noting the remains of the Knights Templar Watergate and the southern city wall, known as the Portwall. The six black granite markers represent the line of this wall. Continue along to Friary and turn right, cross the road, and continue until you have returned to the bottom of the Station incline. Take the pedestrian crossing to the opposite side of Temple Gate noticing on your left, the public house called 'The Reckless Engineer' (a nickname for Brunel). Looking back across the road, the façade of the Brunel terminus can be seen. It was symmetrical when built though the left hand portal had a clock. The right hand portal was demolished when the incline was built.

Rivergate

Carriages entered through the left hand portal and exited through the right. Passengers had to dismount from their carriages and climb stairs to the train shed. This apparent inconvenience was caused by the railway having to be built high enough to clear the river, hence the present day incline. The harbour railway, which closed in 1964, emerged to the left of the façade and continued across Temple Gate on a bridge (now demolished) and along Redcliffe Way,

Move on to Redcliffe Mead Lane and walk up to Prewett Street. The remains of Bristol's last glass cone, which was constructed in the late 18th century, can now be seen as part of a hotel restaurant. This was latterly used as a chemical works and was preserved as part of the hotel in 1973. You are now walking almost parallel to the line of the Bristol Harbour Railway constructed in 1872 as a broad gauge railway.

The glass cones and Bristol Harbour Railway c.1890
Courtesy Bristol Museums Galleries and Archives

The preserved Glass Cone

A little way up the street turn left into a lane leading to a view of the Harbour Railway tunnel driven through the Redcliffe. The space adjacent to the entrance was a coal siding.

Lane off Prewett St leading to railway tunnel

Redcliffe Railway Tunnel

Move on to Colston Parade where on the left can be seen Fry's Almshouse provided by William Fry, a distiller, to accommodate respectable, sober women.

Frys Alms House

Further on is a plaque commemorating the birthplace of Samuel Plimsoll.

Plaque commemorating Samuel Plimsoll

To the right looking into the churchyard is a tram rail relic of wartime blitz damage, left where it landed and commemorated with a plaque.

Tramline buried in air raid

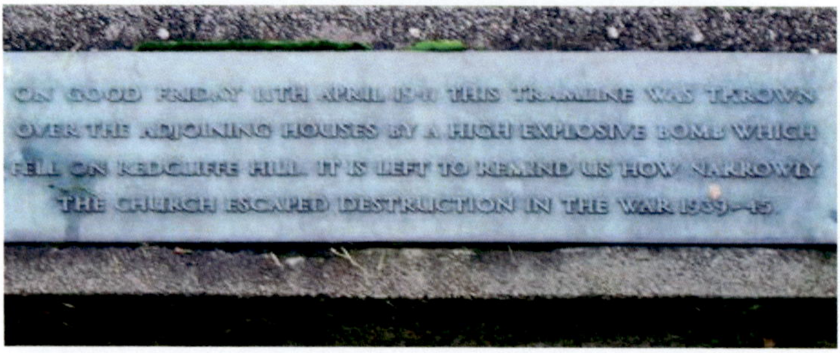

Tramline Plaque

At the end of the parade turn right and pause on the corner to imagine William Watts' Shot Tower in the left hand dual carriageway. Watts developed a new technique for producing lead shot by dropping molten lead through a sieve into water from a height. He made a fortune but sold the business to build houses in Clifton. Difficult building site conditions resulted in his bankruptcy.

Watt's Shot Tower demolished for road widening

Walk down Redcliffe Hill towards the pedestrian crossing where in the wall adjacent to St. Mary Redcliffe Church, one of Bristol's earliest water supplies can be seen, this was provided by Robert de Berkeley in the 1100s.

One of Bristol's early water supplies

The Hermit's Cave

Cross the road, using the pedestrian crossing. Off to the left is the former Quakers Burial Ground, now a park. In the far corner is the site of the hermitage of St. John the Baptist, which links into Redcliffe Caves. Next walk up Redcliffe Hill and turn right into Redcliffe Parade noting the fine Georgian Terrace on the left and on the right a view across the floating harbour to The Grove. At the right hand end of The Grove is Severnshed, built in 1864 and the oldest surviving dock shed.

Severnshed

Turn right, at the incline, and go down to the quayside where there is a gate through which access to Redcliffe Caves is possible. The caves were excavated by the Bristol glass industry.

Entrance to Redcliffe Caves

The Redcliffe was formerly known as Addercliffe. On the left can be seen the fire station, formerly used by the Bristol Fire Brigade as their quayside location adjacent to their fire float mooring.

Docks Fire Station

Former River Police Station

Looking across the water an inlet can be seen under the former River Police Station, the police patrol boats were moored there. Next, walk along the quayside, bearing round to the left at the end, to the Ostrich public house. Just past the Ostrich public house the other end of the tunnel viewed in Prewett Street can be seen.

End of Harbour Railway tunnel

In the roadway the remains of the dual gauge rails can be seen.

Cross the swing bridge built across the Bathurst Basin junction lock. This was formerly a bascule bridge which carried the harbour railway across the lock. While crossing the bridge there is a view of Bathurst Basin on the left. Bathurst Basin was a ship entrance to the upper harbour, closed off to the New Cut at the start of the Second World War; it was constructed at the site of Trin Mill with William Jessop's 1805-1809 Floating Harbour project and was the first part of the Floating Harbour to be opened.

Bathurst Basin, at the far end the former entrance to the New Cut

Bathurst Basin entrance in its working days
Courtesy Bristol Museums Galleries and Archives

Continue around the quayside to Wapping Road noting, on your right, the Italianate engine house used to operate the Prince St. swing bridge, then cross to Princes Wharf where on the end of L shed there is a plaque commemorating the building of Brunel's PS Great Western, which was built on the site in Patterson's Dockyard. Turn to look at Prince St Bridge and note how the harbour is narrowed at this point – this was the site of a gate which separated the lower and upper harbours when the harbour was constructed.

Prince St Bridge (harbour narrowed)

Looking across the water Bush House, constructed in 1831 can be seen. It was occupied by Acraman, Bush, Castle and Co's iron foundry. The building was extended to the north in 1825, increasing its size by around two thirds, in the hope of attracting the tea trade when the East India Co's. monopoly expired. The extension resulted in a tremendous increase in rateable value which bankrupted the Acramans. It was then taken over by J R Bush and became known as the Bush Tea Warehouse, though it probably never handled tea. It now houses the Arnolfini Gallery and offices. In front of the building, sitting on the quayside a representation of a pensive looking John Cabot can be seen.

The Bush Tea Warehouse

A representation of John Cabot

Move carefully on along the quay noting the Museums' three vintage boats and watching out for the gaps in the railway lines, pass, on the right, the electric cranes erected by Stothert and Pitt in 1952. The first three were erected to lift two tons and were upgraded to three tons when the Bristol Steam Navigation Company started to bring in Guinness in vats. The fourth one lifts ten tons. The cranes fell into disuse in 1975 when the dock closed to shipping but have now been, or are being, restored to full working order by Museum Volunteers. On the left, is the entrance to M Shed, Bristol's new museum of industrial and social history.

Looking across the water there is a view of St Augustine's Reach (marred by the construction of the very useful Pero's Bridge) which was created by the diversion of the River Frome in 1215, around one third of a mile from where it joined the River Avon near Bristol Bridge. This gave improved quayside moorings for ships into the City Centre. However, when Jessop's Floating Harbour was created in 1809, tidal movement along the waterway ceased and whilst there was still some flow, sewage from overhanging privies along the river built up and led to silting and unpleasant smells. To overcome this problem, in 1825, the Frome was dammed near Stone Bridge and Mylne's Culvert was constructed to carry the Frome with its noxious contents out to the New Cut. The river now only flows into the Reach when in spate. Moving on along we come to the Guinness Shed, now the Art Warehouse and a building lying back slightly from the rest, which was built with air conditioning to house the Guinness vats, known as the Guinness Cells.

Sketch of Bristol's Principal Waterways in the Late 1800s

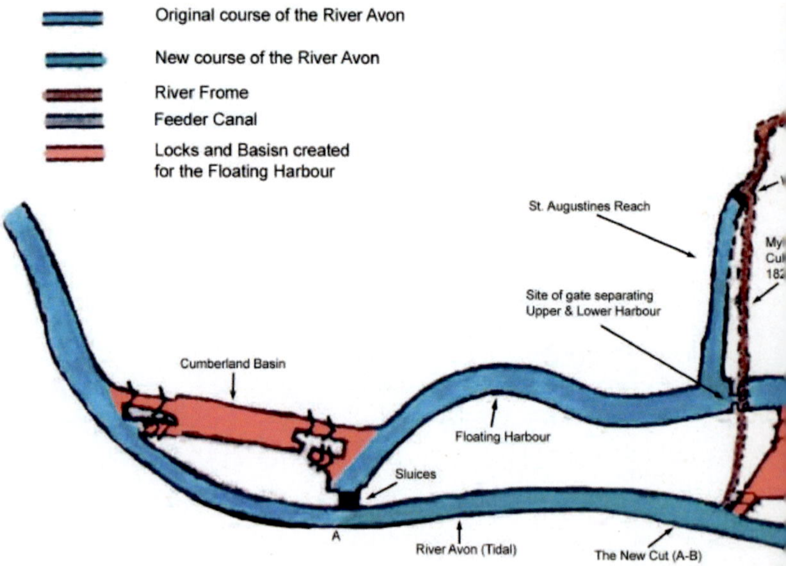

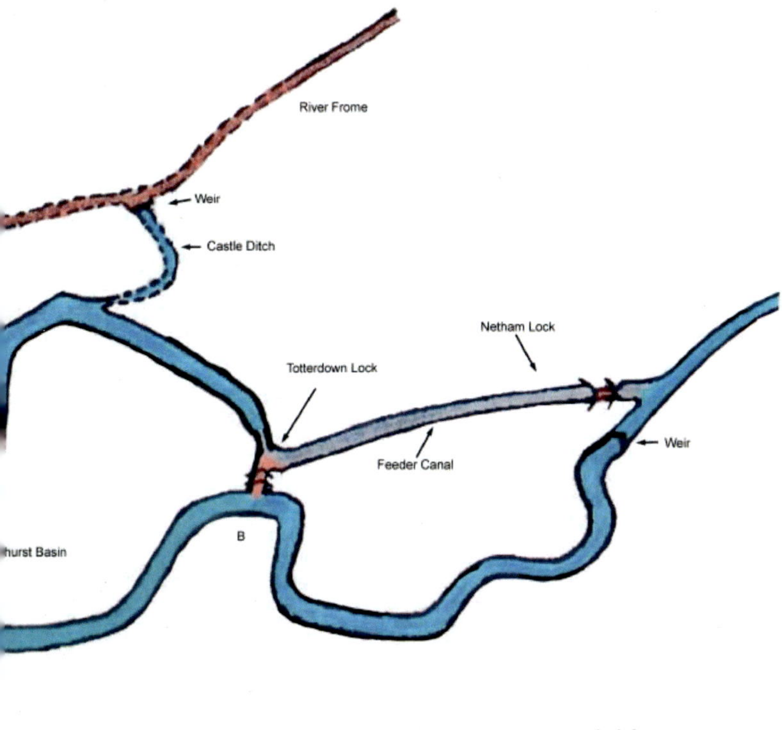
River Frome
Weir
Castle Ditch
Netham Lock
Totterdown Lock
Weir
Feeder Canal
B
hurst Basin

The Guinness Cells

Further on is the Stothert and Pitt, Fairbairn designed, steam crane, built in 1878, and still certified to lift 35 tons. A small portion of the harbour railway has been preserved by the Museum Service, from Princes wharf to the Create Centre, and the Great Western Dockyard. At the approximate site of the steam crane a branch of the Bristol Harbour Railway veers off to the left and runs alongside the New Cut where it joined the main line at Ashton Meadows, the quayside line continues to the Great Western Dockyard.

Fairbairn Steam crane

We have now moved on to Wapping Wharf and come to the final home of Brunel's SS Great Britain and recently, the home of the new Brunel Institute (accessed via the shop on the left hand side of the entrance to the Great Britain).

SS Great Britain at Great Western Dockyard

Here, follow the Harbourside Walk signs to skirt around the Great Western Dockyard and then the Albion dockyard where the last working dry dock in Bristol can be seen. From the Marina, rejoin the quay at Baltic wharf, the site of former timber yards. The timber yards were previously individually named and from the Dockyard were: - Chatham, Gefle, Canada, Cumberland, Onega and Baltic. Further along is what is now known as the Underfall Yard, an area created by William Jessop during the 1805-1809 scheme to construct the Floating Harbour, i.e. where ships could remain afloat at all states of the tide, thus obviating many complaints from ship's masters and merchants when their ships grounded at low tide and sometimes suffered damage.

The rebuilt Medway Queen in the Dry Dock

The area was created by constructing a dam at a junction point where the River Avon and the newly created 'New Cut' joined together. Two sluices were provided; one to control the level of the harbour and the other at low level, to provide scouring for the removal of silt. The dam or overfall provided a continuous flow of water through the Harbour. Another of the functions of the sluices was to "rapidly lower the level of water in the Harbour to break ice and then raise the level to carry the ice across the overfall".*

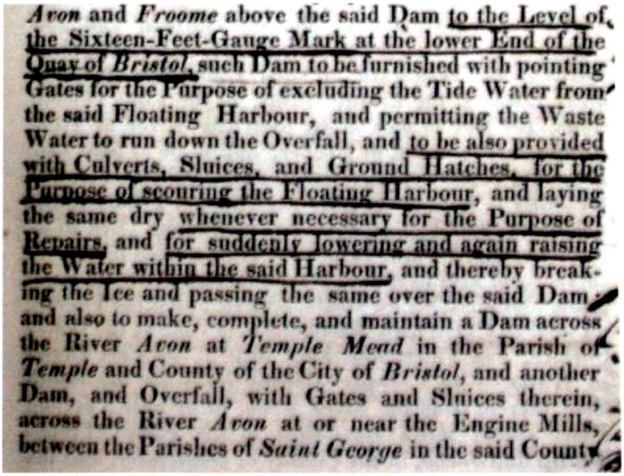

Avon and *Froome* above the said Dam to the Level of the Sixteen-Feet-Gauge Mark at the lower End of the Quay of *Bristol*, such Dam to be furnished with pointing Gates for the Purpose of excluding the Tide Water from the said Floating Harbour, and permitting the Waste Water to run down the Overfall, and to be also provided with Culverts, Sluices, and Ground Hatches, for the Purpose of scouring the Floating Harbour, and laying the same dry whenever necessary for the Purpose of Repairs, and for suddenly lowering and again raising the Water within the said Harbour, and thereby breaking the Ice and passing the same over the said Dam; and also to make, complete, and maintain a Dam across the River *Avon* at *Temple Mead* in the Parish of *Temple* and County of the City of *Bristol*, and another Dam, and Overfall, with Gates and Sluices therein, across the River *Avon* at or near the Engine Mills, between the Parishes of *Saint George* in the said County

**Annotated extract from 1803 Parliamentary Enabling Act*
Courtesy Bristol Central Library

The New Cut worked as a tidal by-pass and extended one mile to Netham, where a dam was provided to hold back the River Avon and provide a head of water to feed a newly created Feeder Canal. The Feeder Canal allowed barge traffic access to the dock and provided water for a flow through the Harbour to the overfall and to make good locking losses. A lock was also provided at Totterdown, where the new cut re-joined the original course of the River Avon, to allow barge entrance. This was closed off in the Second World War.

Considerable build up of silt occurred and in 1832 Brunel was asked for recommendations to clear the problem. He suggested raising the dam at Netham by one foot to increase water flow through the harbour, provide a sluice in the wall at Prince Street Bridge where the Harbour narrowed and provide a mud scraper. No action was taken on these suggestions and in 1840 Brunel did something completely different. He modified the lower scouring sluice by digging what he called

The Overfall, Rowbothom, 1827

Courtesy Bristol City Museums, Galleries & Archives

his 'trunk', a timber lined trench in front of the sluice to create a sort of venturi effect, and this together with a mud scraper improved the situation. The sluices were substantially refurbished in 1900 and augmented by two additional ones, to assist with flood control. This followed an earlier proposal, in 1890, by John Ward Girdlestone. They are now computer controlled.

It is believed that the Overfall remained until the late 1840s/ early 50s when land was reclaimed.

Move on now past the sluice houses, Harbourmasters Office, and Engineer's workshops. The Port Authority's workshops were established here in the 1880s and in the red-brick buildings there is a twin-cylinder steam engine by Tangye of Birmingham and a variety of machines driven by flat belts from line shafting.

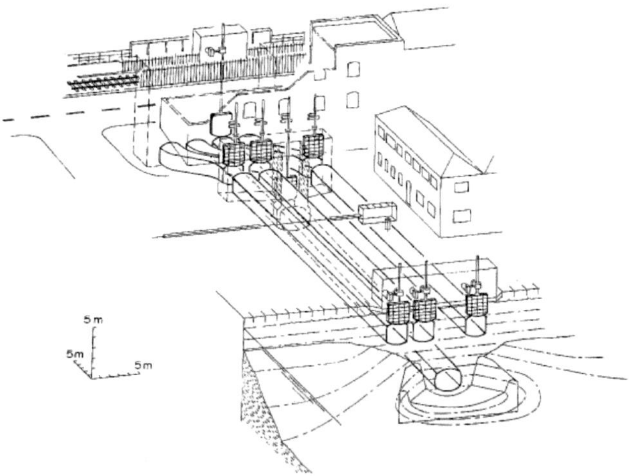

Present Arrangement of sluices at the underfall.

BD6, A later version of Brunel's mud scraper'
Courtesy Bristol Museums Galleries and Archives

Though the engine's boiler is no longer serviceable the engine can be run by compressed air. The underfall Yard is now a scheduled Ancient Monument and is run by the Underfall Yard Trust.

Underfall Yard

Then on to the boatbuilding workshops and blacksmith's shop, run by a cooperative, to the restored Patent Slip initially provided in the 1850s.

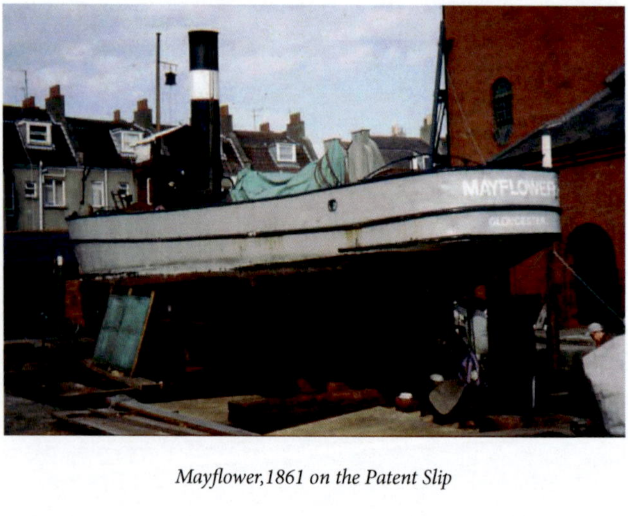

Mayflower,1861 on the Patent Slip

Next along from the Patent Slip, to the left, is the hydraulic engine or pump house with its accumulator tower and a replacement external accumulator provided adjacent to the building, when the one in the brick tower suffered damage.

The Pump House

Hydraulic equipment was installed at the Underfall in the 1880s to replace Howard's original installation by the new junction lock. Two sets of Worthington steam engines supplied the power, and the hydraulic system operated bridges, cranes and lock gates throughout the harbour at a pressure of 750 psi. These engines were replaced by electrical equipment in 1908: this equipment and the accumulator tower have recently been superseded by a new oil hydraulic system.

Move along now to the gates and turn left to Avon Crescent where the houses on the left bear number plates showing that the houses belonged to the Bristol Port Authority e.g. BD8 (Bristol Docks No.8). The building on the opposite side of the road is an electricity sub-station.

Now on to the 'Nova Scotia' public house where, opposite, you can see the original Junction Lock, now dammed, and through which Brunel's SS Great Britain had to pass to go to sea. The lock was 45ft across and the SS Great Britain somewhat wider. This resulted in a very long wait for a high enough spring tide to float her through, with considerable demolition work required on the lock copings and mountings. The slightly incongruous corrugated iron clad sheds house the new hydraulic pumps which operate the bridge and locks.

Original Junction Lock

Cross the road and proceed along Brunel Lock Road, parallel with the waterfront: you are now alongside Cumberland Basin, the main entrance to the Floating Harbour. The basin has undergone three main phases of development. It was planned by William Jessop with four locks, but built with only three, one southern junction and two northern and southern entrance locks from the river to the basin. In the 1840s I K Brunel made substantial alterations to the southern entrance lock, and also built a bridge to span it. Further changes were made in the 1870s when Thomas Howard built a new northern entrance lock to replace Jessop's and added a second junction lock to the north of the first. Remains of all three phases will be seen on the walk.

Cumberland Basin, showing Brunel's lock and tubular construction bridge, towards the top the original northern entrance lock can be seen.

Courtesy of Bristol Museums Galleries and Archives.

Before continuing, note the interesting bollards bearing the maker's name: several different types are to be found in the Cumberland Basin area.

Walk around the side of the city Record Office

Walk across the road and head toward the right hand side of the warehouse building, which now houses the city's Record Office and Create Centre. Turn left, here you can see the tidal River Avon leading to the New Cut and a little further on the Ashton Swing Bridge, which brought the Great Western Railway's lines to the western end of the City Docks and Canons Marsh Goods Station in 1906. This bridge formerly had a top deck carrying a road and a signal box.

Ashton Swing Bridge

The present end of the Harbour Railway

The three red brick Tobacco Bonds were built by the local firm of Cowlins between 1905-1919 and are early examples of buildings with steel and reinforced concrete frames. Retrace your steps and continue along the waterside to the plinth which commemorates the opening of the Plimsoll Bridge and associated road schemes in 1965. The site of the demolished Dock Master's House is close by.

Retrace your steps and continue along the waterside.

From this vantage point there is a fine view of Clifton Suspension Bridge, designed by Brunel but only completed after his death in 1859.

The Clifton Suspension Bridge.

Immediately below it on the Clifton side there formerly stood the Bristol Port Railway & Pier Co's Hotwells Station (closed in 1922), the Tram Terminus for cars on the Brislington route (discontinued in 1938) and the Hotwells Spa. Pleasure steamers formerly tied up at the Jetty and the funicular Clifton Rocks Railway carried people up and down the cliff until 1934. Across the river are the remains of Clifton Bridge Station on the former broad-gauge Portishead line, and at low tide you can see the approaches to Rownham Ferry, moved upstream to this point as a result of the 1870s improvements and closed in 1932.

Rownham Ferry Slips

Continue along the path towards Brunel Lock Road, but instead of rejoining the road, turn sharp left across the bridge. Immediately below you is what was originally Jessop's 33ft wide southern entrance lock, later rebuilt by Brunel to a width of 54ft and given a distinctive U-shaped profile with single hinged gates of wrought-iron which swung back into recesses in the wall: these were operated by means of a capstan which still stands alongside the lock. It has been known as Brunel Lock since the rebuilding. At the same time, Brunel constructed a swing bridge to span his new lock, using the technique of tubular girders made of wrought-iron plates, later incorporated into his Chepstow and Saltash Bridges. This swing bridge survives and is adjacent to the new northern entrance lock.

Brunel's Swing Bridge

This permanently fixed bridge on which you are standing is an identical replica of Brunel's bridge dating from the Howard era of the 1870s. It is hoped that in the future the Brunel Bridge will be restored to full working order as a pedestrian and cycle route across the harbour. Just beyond Brunel Lock is all that remains of Jessop's original Northern Entrance Lock, used as the site for the Gridiron, which was installed in 1884, on which ships could receive minor repairs at low tide (now disused). Note how narrow the island between the two original entrance locks must have been.

Keeping well away from the water's edge, walk across to Thomas Howard's Northern Entrance Lock of the 1870s, and the only one still in use as a lock today. It is 350ft long and 62ft wide, compared to Jessop's 200ft by 45ft. It also brought the added advantages of a more favourable angle of approach from the river and a much larger island between the entrance locks. The north side of the lock can be reached by using the spiral staircases, remaining on the same side of the road on the Plimsoll Bridge itself. Interesting views of the Cumberland Basin can be enjoyed from the Plimsoll Bridge and also from the new pedestrian footbridge to the north of this lock, but the finest view of all is to be had from Rownham Hill, on the other side of the river.

Prince Ivanhoe on Gridiron

View from the pedestrian bridge

From this point, walk back under the Plimsoll Bridge and along Cumberland Basin Road to the eastern end of the basin. Cross Merchants Road and pass through a gap in the wall and you will be alongside the Junction Lock added by Howard in the 1870s, and built to the same dimensions as his new entrance lock. It is spanned by the girder-type Cumberland Basin Swing Bridge, erected in 1925, with steelwork by Lysaghts. Adjacent to the lock on the left hand side is an Italianate Hydraulic Engine House built by Howard to house steam plant when he introduced hydraulic power to the basin.

The Old Pump House

Note also the bridge abutments where the Canons Marsh branch once crossed the lock by means of a swing bridge. Looking towards the city there is, on the left hand side, the site of the now filled-in Merchants Dock, an early wet-dock once owned by the local industrialist William Champion, and beyond it Pooles Wharf, once the G.K. Stothert Dockyard.

Note the two picturesque rows of Dock Cottages - that nearest the road dated 1831. Now the headquarters of the Sea Cadets.

This concludes the walk. BIAS Walks No 2 will continue from this point.

Pooles Wharf showing the empty shipbuilding dry dock and in the foreground Merchants Dock which Stotherts used for fitting out their ships. Courtesy Museum of Bath at Work

Old Dock Cottages

Sources :

- Unless otherwise stated, all photographs by Ken and Valerie Andrews
- Peter Malpass & Andy King, *Bristol's Floating Harbour: 'The first 200 Years'*, Redcliffe Press, 2009
- BIAS Walkabouts
- Docks Committee Minutes, Bristol Record Office
- Bristol Central Library, Bristol Docks Acts